AF266575

KALINKA

АХ, ПОД СОСНОЮ,
AAH, PAD SASNOYU,
DOWN UNDER THE PINE TREES,

ПОД ЗЕЛЕНОЮ
Pad zelenoyu,
DOWN UNDER THE PINE TREES,

спать положите вы меня!
Spat' palazhite, Vee menya!
Sing me sweetly down to sleep!

АЙ-ЛЮЛИ, ЛЮЛИ,
AY - LYULI-LYULI,

АЙ—ЛЮЛИ, ЛЮЛИ,
AY - LYULI-LYULI,

спать положите вы меня!
Spat' palazhite, Vee menya!
Sing me sweetly down to sleep!

КАЛИНКА,
KALINKA,
KALINKA,

КАЛИНКА,
KALINKA,
KALINKA,

КАЛИНКА МОЯ!
KALINKA MOYA!
KALINKA SO TART!

В САДУ ЯГОДА МАЛИНКА,
V SADU YAGADA MALINKA
YOU'RE THE FRUIT, YOU'RE THE FRUIT,

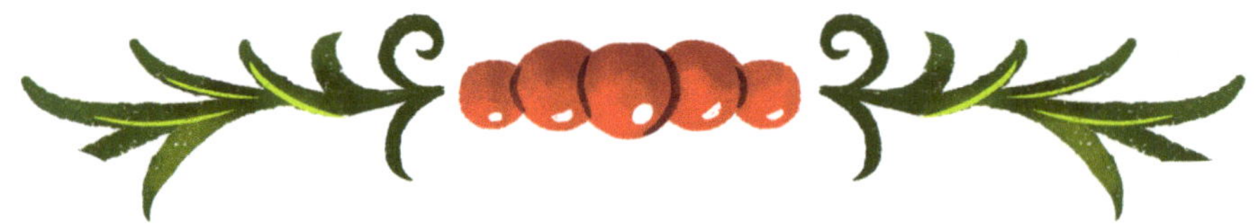

МАЛИНКА МОЯ!
MALINKA MOYA!
YOU'RE THE FRUIT OF MY HEART!

KALINKA

TRANSLATED BY PHILLIP BERMAN AND ZAURE VUK

RUSSIAN TRADITIONAL

9
G⁷
Cm
G⁷
Cm
LIN-KA KA-LIN-KA KA-LIN-KA MA-YA V'SA-DU YA-GODA MA-LIN-KA MA-LIN-KA MA-YA. KA-
LIN-KA, KA-LIN-KA KA-LIN-KA SO TART, YOU'RE THE FRUIT, YOU'RE THE FRUIT, YOU'RE THE FRUIT OF MY HEART! KA
ACCELERANDO

13
G⁷
Cm
G⁷
Cm
LIN-KA KA-LIN-KA KA-LIN-KA MA-YA V'SA-DU YA-GODA MA-LIN-KA MA-LIN-KA MA-YA
LIN-KA, KA-LIN-KA KA-LIN-KA SO TART, YOU'RE THE FRUIT, YOU'RE THE FRUIT, YOU'RE THE FRUIT OF MY HEART!